WESTONBIRT

A CELEBRATION OF THE SEASONS

Best Wishes.

Tony Russell

May 1995

To Rosemary .... Thank you.   T.R.

To Esther .... Timothy .... Tara.   D.H.

WESTONBIRT

A CELEBRATION OF THE SEASONS

Foreword by **H.R.H. The Prince of Wales**

Photography by **Derek Harris**   *Text by* **Tony Russell**

First Published in 1995
by

WoodLand
Publishing

4 Wakerley Court, Wakerley, Oakham, Leicestershire. LE15 8PA

Photography Copyright   Derek Harris.

Text Copyright   Tony Russell.

ISBN   1 899803 00 9

Designed by Derek Harris and Associates Limited.

Origination and Film Sets by Goodfellow & Egan Ltd. Peterborough.

Printed and Bound in Great Britain by Butler and Tanner Ltd. Frome.

Pictures used in this book and other work by Derek Harris is available from
WoodLand and Garden Picture Library
4 Wakerley Court, Wakerley, Oakham, Leicestershire. LE15 8PA.
Telephone 01572 747588. Fax. 01572 747588.

Introduction Pictures

1 *Summer seat in Old Acer Glade.*
2 *A misty morning on The Downs.*
7 *Autumn canopy in Old Acer Glade.*
8 *Carpet of dandelions in the Oak Collection.*
10/27 *Celebration of the Seasons.*

CONTENTS

Now the north wind ceases,
The warm south-west awakes
The heavens are out in fleeces
And the earth's green banner shakes

G. Meredith

Down the hedge a large lime tree teemed with
scent that seemed almost like a voice speaking. It
startled him. He caught a breath of the over sweet
fragrance, then stood still, listening expectantly.

D. H. Lawrence

CONTENTS

*It was a foggy morning, and the trees shed in noisy
water drops the moisture they had collected from
the thick air, an acorn occasionally falling from its
cup to the ground, in company with the dripping.
In the meads, sheets of spider's-web, almost opaque
with wet, hung in folds over the fences, and the
falling leaves appeared in every variety of brown,
green and yellow hue.*

Thomas Hardy

*Oh, I remember now
A dell of snow,
Frost on the bough;
None there but I:
Snow, snow, and a wintry sky.*

Walter de la Mare

H.R.H. The Prince of Wales
ST. JAMES'S PALACE

I visited Westonbirt for the first time in 1982 and immediately fell under its spell. To walk around the beautifully landscaped grounds, surrounded by some of the tallest, oldest and, indeed, rarest trees of their kind in the world is a great delight. One can marvel at the foresight of Robert Holford who started this remarkable collection in 1829.

I have returned to Westonbirt many times since that first visit, and have found much to inspire me for my own plantings nearby at Highgrove. Holford began planting on a bare Cotswold field and, in some ways, that is what I have done myself, although he had the advantage of coinciding with a wonderful patch of greensand which I did not! It required a good deal of faith, but I am sure Holford would feel entirely justified if he knew how wonderfully well his creation had fared, and how much pleasure it now gives.

Autumn in this part of Gloucestershire always brings a sudden influx of visitors to the area, all with the singular, and admirable, intention of seeing Westonbirt trees in full Autumn colour. The displays are quite magnificent, particularly from the Japanese Maples which are planted in their hundreds. Those of us who live close by also take the opportunity to see Westonbirt at other times of the year. It is without doubt, a garden for all seasons, and a visit on any day is bound to lift the spirits.

This splendid book describes and depicts Westonbirt in all its glory, and at all seasons, and I believe it will be welcomed as much by those who have not yet visited as by those who already know and love this very special corner of Gloucestershire.

9

8.

THE SPIRIT OF WESTONBIRT

One cold late November afternoon I was making my way back through Silk Wood towards the warmth of my office. I had spent the afternoon selecting planting sites for some tender Eucalyptus which had been grown in the Propagation Unit and were now ready to be planted out.

As I turned onto Waste Drive I could see ahead of me, two people standing quite silently with heads bowed. As I approached, one of them, a man in his sixties looked up and smiled. "Excuse us", he said, "we're just having a couple of minutes contemplation".

I smiled and apologised for disturbing them, "You haven't", said the woman with him, "we were just saying how quickly the night is coming in, we should be getting back".

They turned towards me and the three of us set off together down the drive towards Waste Gate just visible through the November dusk.

"We often come here to think", she continued, "we've been to the hospital this afternoon to see our first grandchild and came on to Westonbirt to say thank you for such a lovely baby". "You see", said the man, obviously feeling he should explain further, "Westonbirt is like a church to us, the beauty and serenity we find here allows us to see things more clearly. It helps us to understand things that happen to us, or to others come to that. We came here last Saturday after hearing of the dreadful bombing in that shopping centre".

We chatted on until reaching the arboretum offices, they continuing on towards their car, I towards the patch of light from my office window.

Their explanation had not been necessary, they like so many others had been touched by the Westonbirt spirit. For Westonbirt is not simply one of the greatest collections of trees and shrubs ever put together by man, as grand as this may sound, there is still much more to the place. There

is a vibrancy, a living breathing soul that exudes from every leaf and bower.

Rich dark leaf mould lying thickly beneath ancient oaks seems to heave rhythmically like some great creature in slumber. Stirring in springtime to push up great swathes of wild flowers across its body and in autumn to draw back into itself a storehouse of nourishment ready for next year's re-birth.

You can feel its presence as you wander through Westonbirt's woods and at times part of the essence will come back to you, like a familiar childhood memory, when you are far away from Westonbirt in mind and body.

This book attempts through words and photographs to borrow some of that spirit, it would be impossible to capture it, we are-after all mere mortals. We have written and photographed throughout the year whilst the feelings of each season are around and within us. For Westonbirt is a place to visit at any time of year not just in autumn when the maples catch fire, each month has its own special treasures. It can be a particular flower, such as the sulphur yellow, witch hazel in January or the way the February light surrounds the expanding birch buds with a purple haze, or even the echoing call of a cock pheasant on a hollow dark November afternoon.

If on that November afternoon you go indoors, sit by the fire with this book, and for an hour find again those heady ripe days of high summer. Hear pine cones crack open like pistols and see the great dome of Westonbirt House shimmering a mile away above the backs of cattle on The Downs.

If on that November afternoon you feel again that rush of excitement as you discover the first primrose of spring, then we have achieved our objective. To pass on a little of the spirit of Westonbirt.

28. Waste Drive in spring.

SPRING

Now the north wind ceases,
The warm south-west awakes
The heavens are out in fleeces
And the earth's green banner shakes
G. Meredith

30. A spring morning on Main Drive.

Overleaf 29. Rhododendrons and azaleas on Circular Drive.

SPRING – *Flowering Splendour*

As the days grow longer and warmer so Westonbirt begins to stir from its winter slumber. Deep within Silk Wood the first leaves of wild honeysuckle are cautiously unfolding, only too aware that the frost and snow of yesterday could return tomorrow.

Within days other plants follow suit almost as if they have been patiently waiting for the intrepid honeysuckle to begin the performance. Pale yellow catkins drip from every branchlet interspersed with bright red female hazel flowers like little crimson stars.

Willow trees collected from all around the world and now growing contentedly in the sheltered environment of Willow Walk compete for the best display. White, red, yellow, even black catkins sit proudly on leafless branches, for this is their moment and they make the most of it knowing that before too long they will be eclipsed by the grander displays of rhododendron, camellia and magnolia.

On the edge of the wood a dormouse, woken from hibernation, drops from his aerial roadway high in the hazel canopy landing in a carpet of snowdrops, his progress indicated by delicately nodding, white petalled heads as he scurries back into the woodland. Startled, no doubt, by the sound of the woodsman's billhook coming down with an echoing thud as another hazel stem is coppiced.

Silk Wood is old, there have been trees on this site since the end of the last ice age some 12,000 years ago. The art of coppicing, or cutting trees down to the ground and allowing them to regrow, was practised by Neolithic man. In Silk Wood the scene on this early spring morning would have changed little in the last 600 years. Each year an area of hazel is coppiced, after nine years the first area that was coppiced is re-coppiced, with the resulting stems being used to make trellis hurdles, pergolas and rustic furniture. This sympathetic woodland management will hopefully mean little change in the next 600 years. On the area coppiced last year the morning sun is warming up the soil no longer shrouded by the woodland canopy. Clumps of primrose and wood anemone are already in full flower and will be joined by wild garlic, bluebells, early purple orchids and foxgloves by the time May arrives.

There is a timeless quality about Silk Wood, the trials and tribulations of late twentieth century life are forgotten as one wanders beneath great bowers created by ancient oaks whose forebears have stood looking down on the same scene for countless generations. Small-leaved lime trees, believed to be 2000 years old, grow happily alongside a plantation of young larch, which in early spring is a delight to walk through. Graceful straw coloured drooping branches are covered with clusters of purple-pink female flowers, closely followed by soft emerald green tufts as the new foliage starts to emerge.

Close by the larch plantation in Cherry Glade one can almost hear the word 'spring' being whispered by the breeze as it flits around each tree, spring! spring! it breathes as it lightly touches each naked branch urging it into blossom. Sure enough one by one the trees respond. One of the first into flower is *Prunus conradinae*, it has delightful blush white fragrant flowers which cover almost every inch of every branch.

It is soon joined by the Fuji cherry, *Prunus incisa*, a small Japanese cherry with pale pink blossom which has long been used by the Japanese for Bonsai. There is a virtual stampede to be the next into flower, with over 200 different types of cherry at Westonbirt, different ones come into flower every day during March and April. Many are from Japan and China, however one should not forget our native wild cherry, *Prunus avium*. Tucked away on the western fringe of Silk Wood is a wonderful grove of wild cherry trees, walking into this grove for the first time on a warm late April day can be a memorable experience. Long tall pillars of mahogany red bark, peeling and fissured with age topped by clouds of white blossom against a blue sky.

With the profusion of springtime flowers at Westonbirt it can be easy to ignore foliage, however, a stroll through The Link on a sunny spring morning with the sun still low in the sky will change all that. The Link contains majestic old oak trees, some pre-dating the founding of the Arboretum in 1829. Widely spaced they provide dappled shade, ideal conditions for the maples growing beneath. No ordinary maples, these are Japanese maples chosen and planted deliberately to provide a kaleidoscope of autumn colour, but just take a look at them in spring. As each tiny bud opens, delicate foliage starts to unfurl producing an exquisite mosaic of pink, gold, bronze and a thousand different shades of fresh green. Looking closer you will see how leaf shapes differ from tree to tree, some are so finely dissected they remind one of filigree lace, others are broad and palm like, hence the scientific name *Acer palmatum*.

We all have different visions of heaven, mine has to be The Link and its surrounding woodland in May. The caution of early spring is forgotten and one can feel, all around, a tremendous surge of growth as the re-born woodland clothes itself ready for another year. The whole area is carpeted with bluebells, in places almost waist high, and from a distance it seems a hazy purple blue cloud is hovering above the woodland floor. With an almost continual accompaniment of bird song where else could one be but heaven?

There are over 18,000 trees and shrubs at Westonbirt collected from all around the world, and with such an extensive collection there is something in flower every day of the year. It is in spring, however, that flowering reaches a climax. In some areas such as Savill Glade the displays can be breathtaking. It was in Savill Glade that Robert Holford, the founder of the Arboretum planted the first trees in 1829. It is said that he chose this spot after watching badgers working. Realising the soil they removed from their sett was a deep sandy loam he guessed (quite rightly), it would be an ideal medium for growing new plants being introduced into Britain at that time. Westonbirt is in Cotswold country, typically shallow alkaline soil overlying oolithic limestone, so the soil of Savill Glade (and there are other deposits around the Arboretum) is unusual and ideal for growing plants which prefer deep acid soil such as camellia, rhododendron, magnolia and azalea.

Many of us think of these plants as shrubs, however, in their native habitat some have the potential to become large trees. There are, for example, in the foothills of the Himalayas, rhododendron forests and magnolias over 30 metres tall. A visit to Westonbirt in spring will provide more than a hint of that exotic mountainous region. Giant tree rhododendrons abound with great ball-like clusters of pink, red, mauve, purple, white and yellow flowers high above one's head. On Circular and Main Drive flower laden branches droop to the ground, presenting a wall of colour some seven metres tall.

Some of these venerable giants are over 100 years old, planted by Robert Holford's son, Sir George Holford who had a penchant for rhododendrons, cross breeding many to produce new cultivars. This work was considered so sensitive, due to the rarity and value of certain plants, that Sir George had 'secret' nurseries around the Arboretum. Sir George's Glade, close to Savill Glade, is on the site of a secret nursery and here today one can find straight lines of rhododendrons surviving as they were grown in nursery beds some 100 years ago. Many Westonbirt rhododendrons from this period still defy identification, those that are named carry labels to assist the visitor.

There are so many spectacular rhododendrons at Westonbirt that it is difficult to mention just a few, but *Rhododendron fictolacteum* with its creamy-white bell, shaped flowers spotted with crimson is quite magnificent, the underside of its large leaves are covered with a soft cinnamon coloured down. *Rhododendron barbatum* is another, with bright crimson-scarlet flowers and beautiful rusty red peeling bark.

Less showy, but for me the finest of them all, are two species with smaller flowers, *Rhododendron cinnabarinum* with waxy red tubular flowers and *Rhododendron quinquefolium* with pure white flowers spotted with green and exquisite diamond shaped lime green leaves fringed with pink. Both flower in May and lift the soul like no other rhododendron can.

Complementing this extravaganza of colour are the magnolias, Westonbirt has some 50 different types and the variation between species is quite amazing.

One of the earliest to flower is the Goddess magnolia, *Magnolia sprengeri* Diva, considered by some to be one of the loveliest sights in spring. It certainly is one of the most dramatic, the largest specimen in the Arboretum is at the southern end of Savill Glade and can easily be found in early March by the cluster of admiring visitors surrounding its base. Believed to be the tallest in Britain this tree can be covered from top to bottom with hundreds of rose pink flowers which start goblet shaped then gradually open to the size of a tea plate.

Just yards away and in perfect contrast is the 'star' magnolia, *Magnolia stellata*, a shrub more than a tree, it has white fragrant star-like flowers which emerge from a distinctive large hairy grey bud long before the leaves appear. As with all early flowering magnolias their beauty can be fleeting, a sharp spring frost will destroy their spectacular blooms overnight.

Magnolia wilsonii, named after the great Victorian Gloucestershire plant hunter, Ernest Wilson, is far more sensible, it waits until the threat of frost has passed, producing flowers in late May after the leaves have emerged. The wait is worth it, a pendulous flower with thick creamy-white petals set off by crimson stamens in the centre and, oh! what a fragrance. On a warm still late spring afternoon the air is heady with a wonderful scent that wafts around the plant and its neighbours for quite some distance.

In spring it is very easy not to walk far from Savill Glade, the colours and scents are intoxicating, just a few steps can open up entirely new vistas. What could be better than leaning against some ancient trunk watching bumble bees tumble out of purple speckled foxglove throats and every now and then catching, on the breeze, the echoing call of a cuckoo sitting on an oak branch across the valley in Silk Wood.

If you can summon the willpower to walk on, there are other delights to discover in the Arboretum and one to head for is the Sunrise Horse Chestnut. Best approached from Mitchell Drive, this wonderful tree can be seen from 200 metres away as a large salmon pink puffy ball rising from the horizon like the early morning sun. Closer inspection will reveal the colour to be produced by new leaves as they unfurl. Within a few weeks the colour fades and by summer they are green just like the Common Horse Chestnut familiar to us all, but for that short period in spring its beauty is unsurpassed.

Mitchell Drive has a character all of its own, it is much more open than most of the Arboretum and provides wonderful views across the downland separating the old Arboretum from Silk Wood.

Grazed for centuries by sheep and cattle, The Downs in late spring are a haven for wild flowers. Cowslips and the rare oxlip rub shoulders with early purple and pyramidal orchids. Wild flowers are an integral part of Westonbirt, the grass sward is managed to encourage a wide variety from rare species such as green hellebore and the butterfly orchid to primroses and even dandelions which can provide such a magical contrast to bluebells in May.

It is whilst walking on The Downs that one appreciates the size and contrasting landscapes of Westonbirt. To the south and west across a steep sided valley lies Silk Wood with great billowing heads of oak stretching away into the distance. In the foreground, standing like sentries, is a line of old 'battle worn' poplars, scarred and broken limbed from years of combat with wind, rain and snow.

Turning northwards the skyline is punctured by tall spire-like conifers interspersed with broadleaved trees of every shape, colour and texture, an arboreal mosaic depicting one of the finest collections of trees and shrubs in the world.

It wasn't until 1975 that the first full survey of the collection started, it took some seven years to complete and during that time every tree and shrub was mapped, inspected, catalogued and, where possible, identified. Today there are some 18,000 listed specimens within the collection spread throughout almost 600 acres of gentle Cotswold countryside.

Alongside The Downs, indeed at one time an integral part of The Downs, is The Pool, a curious square stone-sided dew pond. It is the only water to be found at Westonbirt, there is no large lake or formal water feature as seen in many of the grand Victorian gardens. All the marvellous vistas and landscapes at Westonbirt have been created by imaginative planting of trees and shrubs using their individual features of form, colour and foliage. The Pool predates the Arboretum and was originally built to provide cattle and sheep with drinking water whilst they grazed the downland. The construction is similar to that of an inverted pyramid, four sloping sides of Cotswold stone, sunk into puddled clay, meet in the centre of the pool some two metres below the surface. It has no underground feed from spring or stream, relying entirely on rainfall and moisture forming on the stones overnight and running back into the pool. The stones also prevent bank erosion, quite often a problem at water holes when a continual procession of animals come to drink.

Even in the driest of springs the water level drops little, thus providing a wonderful haven for wildlife. Frogs, newts and pond skaters abound and in late spring metallic blue damsel flies flit and hover around that most majestic of water plants, the yellow flag *Iris pseudacorus*, standing proudly at the waters edge.

Turning away from The Pool and wandering down Main Drive towards Circular Drive it is not long before a powerful fragrance fills the air. As the sun rises in the sky the scent becomes almost overwhelming. Suddenly almost without warning turning onto Circular Drive one is confronted by a spectacular bank of fragrant deciduous azaleas. Flowers of flame red, orange, apricot, lemon, cream, and white are clustered together in a giant collage depicting the final celebration of spring. For summer has almost arrived at Westonbirt, long still balmy evenings, ideal for badger watching stretch ahead. Honeysuckle, that intrepid plant which heralded the arrival of spring with a flush of soft downy leaves is now twisting and climbing through new hazel growth, leaving in its wake a trail of sweetly scented creamy-white flowers.

On The Downs the grass is knee high, bespotted with wild flower seed heads and the call of the cuckoo no longer echoes across the valley. Farewell to the cuckoo and to spring, we will look eagerly for your return next year.

Overleaf 31-39. Flowering Splendour.

40. Cherry blossom.

41. Early evening in Cherry Glade.

42. Cherry blossom in the Hillier Cherry Glade.

40.

41.

42.

Opposite 43. *A spring morning near Palmer Ride.*

44. *Bluebells beneath the elm collection.*

45. *Spring tranquillity.*

46. *Larch and oak near Broad Drive.*

45.   46.

44.

49.

48.

50.

47-49. *Deciduous azaleas.*

50. *Rhododendrons on Main Drive.*

Opposite   51. *Main Drive rhododendrons.*

47.

53.

54.

55.

56.

57.

58.

59.

60.

61. *Old oaks in Silk Wood.*

62. *Early morning in The Link.*

63. *Wild flowers near Cherry Glade.*

Opposite 64. Betula ermanii *on Mitchell Drive.*

62.

63.

66.

67.

68.

69.

70.

71.

Overleaf 65. *Bluebells and*
dandelions beneath
the Silk Wood maples.

Opposite 66. Magnolia x wieseneri.

67. *Pieris flowers.*

68. *Camellia flowers.*

69. *Magnolia flower.*

70. Stachyurus *flowers.*

71. *Deutzia flowers.*

72. *Magnolia flowers.*

73. *Camellia flowers.*

73.

Opposite 74. *Yellow flags,* Iris pseudacorus, *by the Dew Pond.*

75. *Azaleas and rhododendrons on Pool Avenue.*

76. *Misty morning by the Dew Pond.*

77. *Misty morning with cattle grazing on The Downs.*

78. *Westonbirt School entrance.*

78.

75.

77.

76.

79. *Bluebells on the edge of the Wild Wood.*

80. *Cherry blossom in the morning sun.*

81. *Wild flowers of Silk Wood.*

79.

80.

46

81.

Opposite 82. Tree rhododendrons in Savill Glade.

   83. Bluebells and bark.

   84. The first primrose of spring.

   85. Fallen rhododendron petals amid the bluebells.

Overleaf 86. Heaven?

83.

84.

85.

87. *Waste Drive in summer.*

SUMMER

*Down the hedge a large lime tree teemed with scent
that seemed almost like a voice speaking. It startled
him. He caught a breath of the over sweet fragrance,
then stood still, listening expectantly.*

D. H. Lawrence

89. Late summer on Mitchell Drive.

Overleaf 88. A summer's evening in The Link.

SUMMER – *Tranquil Glades*

By mid-June the urgency of spring has been left far behind. The initial surge of sap that coursed through every plant from giant oak to creeping periwinkle has subsided, replaced by a gentler rhythm that ebbs and flows with the warmth of the sun.

Of all the seasons at Westonbirt it is summer which produces the strongest sense of well being. Peace and tranquillity fall softly about one's shoulders within minutes of entering beneath the luxuriant green canopy. On a hot summer's day walking into the Arboretum from The Downs is like entering some vast green cathedral. It is cool and shady; shafts of dappled sunlight, diffused by a latticework of foliage, colour the woodland floor as if through a giant stained glass window. High above, translucent burgundy leaves of the smoke tree, *Cotinus coggygria*, sway gently back and forth across the sun's path. Moved by a breeze which has run through the ears of acres of corn during its journey across the golden agricultural lands surrounding this arboreal island.

In many ways summer is also the most elusive time of the Westonbirt year. There are no gloriously large colour displays of flower or foliage, or a snow white stage upon which evergreen and dogwood can proudly perform. However, the jewels are there, only more bashful, hiding themselves away amidst millions of leaves, fully expanded to capture the sun's energy for their photosynthetic process. Finding these jewels can be so rewarding, they are like little secrets waiting to be discovered and what a privilege when they reveal themselves to you.

In early summer two worth searching for are the Chilean fire bush, *Embothrium coccineum* and the lantern tree, *Crinodendron hookerianum*. The fire bush originates from South America growing on slopes in the Andes Mountains, where it can grow into a tree some ten metres tall. In Britain it is fairly tender and rarely exceeds a shrubby four metres. Nevertheless, this evergreen plant produces one of the most spectacular summer flower displays at Westonbirt. In a way the flower is reminiscent of honeysuckle, but no honeysuckle produces flowers as big or with such vivid colour.

They are flame red, hence the name fire bush, and indeed from a distance it does look as if each branch is covered with glowing embers. Westonbirt's best specimens are in Savill Glade and not far away on Circular Drive can be found the lantern shaped flowers of *Crinodendron hookerianum*. Again from South America, this plant is also evergreen. The flowers first appear as tiny green capsules in late winter, they gradually expand as spring arrives but it is early summer before they turn a brilliant red, contrasting so well against the dark green leathery leaves. Not unlike a fuchsia flower at first glance, but there the similarity ends, these flowers are strong and waxy and will stay on the plant through soaring temperatures of high summer.

One of the largest exotic trees in Britain is the tulip tree, *Liriodendron tulipifera*. A magnificent tree, originating from North America, it was first introduced into Britain in the 17th century. Today it can be found in many large gardens and parks, and is planted widely as an ornamental tree. The name refers to the shape of the flowers which appear in mid-summer and are tulip like in appearance, greenish yellow in colour with orange markings. Specimens occur throughout Westonbirt, one of the largest is on Willesley Drive, however, the majority are found in the north east corner of the Arboretum making up part of Jackson Avenue.

Jackson Avenue is one of three main avenues which radiates from Westonbirt House and in its day was certainly one of the most majestic. It is comprised of tulip trees, lime trees and cedars and at one time extended far beyond the present Arboretum boundary. The end nearest the house was, until comparatively recently, the main entrance to the Arboretum.

On either side of the heavy ornate entrance gates stands a giant redwood tree, *Sequoiadendron giganteum*, planted by Robert Holford and his wife Mary in 1856. Already over 100 feet tall they are still in their prime, sadly the same cannot be said for Jackson Avenue. Storms and droughts have taken their toll on the tulip and cedar trees in the avenue. Today only the limes give some indication as to its past splendour.

A short stroll from Jackson Avenue is Lime Avenue and the sounds of summer become progressively louder as one approaches. Outside the Arboretum the corn rasps and creaks as the mid-summer sun blazes down. Inside, beneath the canopy of lime trees the air is cool, the shadows strong and the sound quite deafening. Overhead millions of bees methodically gather nectar from blossom produced in vast quantities upon every branch. It is a pale yellow hanging blossom, quite small and yet so powerful. Below upon the sward, bewildered bees stumble, so intoxicated by nectar they have fallen from the canopy. The heavy scent alone is intoxicating but with the accompanying drone from above it is not only bees that fall asleep beneath the limes on hot summer afternoons.

Westonbirt is a wonderful mix of formality and wilderness. Places deep within Silk Wood still retain the essence of ancient woodland. Here one finds a sense of remoteness, a feeling that one might just be the first person ever to stand on a particular spot. To linger here is to be transported back through time, the centuries fall away and with it any cares and worries of modern day life. Gone are roads, cars and computerised communication. Nothing would seem more natural than to be met on one of the Silk Wood tracks by horse and cart driven by a smock clothed rustic.

Speckled wood butterflies dance through dusty shafts of mid-afternoon sunlight filtering through the oak leaf canopy. Their dappled wing pattern replicated on the brown woodland floor where the sunlight comes to rest. Here and there, purple foxglove flowers sway gently in a sultry breeze. The only other movement comes from a procession of wood ants crossing the path on their way to and from their nest of twigs, leaves and pine needles. Almost knee high, this dry heap of vegetation is constantly growing as each ant returns with more leaf debris for the pile. In the tranquillity of Silk Wood the rustle of their activities can be heard a good six metres away.

In contrast, parts of the Old Arboretum are park-like by design. One can almost see the bowed heads of Robert and Sir George Holford, father and son, bent low over the master plan of their pleasure grounds. Deciding exactly where each tree and shrub should be planted and quite probably planting many themselves. Nowhere is this more apparent than on Holford Ride, a long open avenue stretching some 650 metres.

The trees and shrubs planted on both sides along its length read like a botanical dictionary of woody plants from the temperate regions of the world. Not carelessly planted but each one a compliment to its neighbour or the plant on the opposite side of the ride. Two massive spreading hummocks of Persian ironwoods, *Parottia persica*, stand either side of Britain's finest group of incense cedars, *Calocedrus decurrens*. The effect is staggering, made even more so when one remembers that these trees were only waist high when planted more than 80 years ago.

Lime Avenue joins Holford Ride some two thirds along its length. On a hot summer's day emerging from Lime Avenue is like stepping from a darkened auditorium onto a sunlit stage. The stage curtains are two superb groups of giant redwoods, *Sequoiadendron giganteum*, considered by some to be the best examples of redwood groves outside North America.

Close by is a group of Holford Pines, *Pinus x holfordiana*, a hybrid pine produced when two quite different species growing at Westonbirt cross-pollinated around the turn of the century. Seed was collected from one parent, the Mexican white pine, *Pinus ayacahuite*, and the resulting seedling identified and named, as a hybrid in 1933, in recognition of the Holford's influence on Westonbirt.

The cones on the Holford pine can be up to 30cms long and on hot summer days, along with other cones from the hundreds of conifers within the Westonbirt collection, can be heard cracking like pistol shots in the heat. Each crack indicating a loosening of the woody cone scale covering the precious seed inside.

During periods of hot, dry weather, resin will begin to ooze from wounds and fissures in the bark and flow down the stem, branches and cones. A fallen cone discovered by a child at this time of year can be a very sticky treasure indeed. As the resin flows so the air surrounding the tree becomes filled with an aromatic resinous vapour. The increasing strength of the sun ripens this heady scent which is one of the most evocative perfumes of the Westonbirt summer, living on in the mind long after the first frost has turned the resin flow into a white crystallised trail. When the resin flows, so the great domed roof of Westonbirt House, almost a mile away, shimmers and quakes above the backs of cattle grazing rhythmically on The Downs.

The present house was built for Robert Holford between 1863 and 1878 on the site of a Regency gothic house built by his father in 1823. Both Robert and his son Sir George Holford lived in the house whilst continuing to enlarge the Arboretum, Robert died in 1892 and Sir George in 1926. The first trees having been planted in 1829, these two men between them managed Westonbirt throughout a period lasting almost one hundred years. After Sir George's death the estate passed to a nephew, the fourth Lord Morley, who then sold the house and in 1928 it became a private girls school, its interior has changed little since. It is a grade I listed building and great care is taken to preserve its original features. The Morley family continued to own the Arboretum until 1956 when in lieu of death duties it passed to the Government, who in turn handed over its management to the Forestry Commission.

During the years following the Second World War little maintenance had taken place, both staff and money had been in short supply. By the time the Forestry Commission took over there was an urgent need to carry out remedial work in order to try to save as much as possible of this wonderful collection of trees and shrubs.

By the mid-1960s this had been achieved and attention turned to creating major new features in the Holford landscaping tradition. Three of these features, Leyshon Avenue (otherwise known as the New Acer Glade), The Link and Palmer Ride, have already become major attractions for visitors to Westonbirt and will continue to be for future generations. Time scales are long at Westonbirt, the Arboretum has developed gradually over 165 years. Foresters managing the Arboretum today are working to continue this marvellous collection into the twenty first century and beyond. At the same time they are constantly aware of the need to maintain the existing collection on a daily basis, thus ensuring survival for some of the most endangered tree and shrub species in the world.

By mid-summer the first swallows to arrive at Westonbirt have paired and are raising their first brood. Every evening in good weather they fly low catching insects on the wing. Returning time and again to young who cry frantically from their nest of mud and grass, amongst the rafters of outbuildings surrounding Keepers Cottage. The walls of the cottage stay warm well into evening, each Cotswold stone slowly releasing to the evening air heat absorbed during the long hot summer day.

Long after dusk, plants growing against the cottage walls such as *Magnolia grandiflora*, bask in this radiation and the sweet perfume of a Kiftsgate rose fills the cottage garden.

As darkness rushes in, the swallows are replaced by pippestrelle and horseshoe bats flitting and swooping around the outbuildings and greenhouses. In the distance a tawny owl calls, to be answered seconds later by another, this time much closer, possibly in the old pollarded oak tree by the side of the Visitor Centre. It is now that many Westonbirt creatures are just beginning their night time activities. Hunting for food and water or, in the case of the badger cubs in the sett close to Pool Avenue, it is time to have some fun. Having been born in late February they are now four months old and at their most playful.

A favourite game is 'king of the castle', they find a high point, perhaps a heap of soil smoothed by many other nights play and proceed to knock each other off the top. Gradually they become excited, playful fights break out with much yelping and biting. A large hemlock tree becomes the centre of their play area as they chase each other around the base. On warm still nights a pungent musk like scent fills the air, secreted by the cubs as they excitedly play. Some nights they will play for hours stopping only to drink from The Pool or to search out a juicy earthworm. On other nights, play might be interrupted, perhaps when a dog fox crossing the Downs close to the sett lets out a series of three hoarse barks. He is no threat to the badgers, simply out searching for food to take back to his vixen and cubs in a den on the edge of Silk Wood. Nevertheless, for a while they stay just inside the sett entrance, the white central stripe on their heads just visible every now and then as they move across the beams from the large summer moon.

A warm summer moonlit night in the Arboretum can be quite magical. The moon casts strange shadows and lights up night time glades and plants which are virtually ignored by the sun. One tree, magnificent day or night is *Davidia involucrata*, this has a number of names including the pocket handkerchief tree and dove tree. It is however its third name that immediately springs to mind when seen at night, the 'ghost tree'. Standing on the edge of Main Drive, the largest specimen in Britain appears to float above the ground, held there by a flock of ghostly white doves. Every year at the beginning of summer visitors to Westonbirt arrive specifically to pay homage and to marvel at the ghost tree in flower. These flowers are actually small, dark and fairly inconspicuous, however they are clothed by a pair of large white bracts, protective leaf-like sheaths, which hang down from every branch, fluttering in the slightest breeze. It is these bracts which produce such a strange effect beneath the moon's spotlight gaze.

As summer heads towards its zenith, around the time one feels sure it will last forever, so the hydrangea flowers appear. Hydrangeas have suffered over the years due to urbanisation, planted widely in towns and parks with little thought for landscaping. However, in the right setting they can provide a superb summer flower display. Such a setting is Victory Glade, a lovely leafy glade surrounded by towering Douglas fir and sweet chestnut. Here in high summer can be found great clumps of hydrangeas with flowers from pure white through to royal blue. One of my favourites, *Hydrangea aspera*, it carries magnificent heads of pale porcelain - blue flowers in some instances as large as a football. After the searing heat of Main Drive this particular group reminds me of a cool shady pool, they will still be flowering when the first frost of autumn arrives. Another lovely plant is *Hydrangea heteromalla* 'Bretschneideri', more commonly called white lacecap it has the added attraction of rusty brown peeling bark.

Quite different to the hydrangeas but just as beautiful are the eucryphias. They have white nodding flowers with conspicuous stamens that give off such a charming fragrance. Eucryphias flower at a time when most plants are beginning to think of autumn and this makes them such a special delight. One of the finest is *Eucryphia x nymansensis*, raised in 1915 at Nymans, the famous garden in Sussex. It attracts bees by the thousand in those last few frantic, nectar seeking weeks of summer.

Throughout the summer members of the *Sorbus* family, which includes our native rowan, *Sorbus aucuparia*, have been quietly waiting for their moment to perform. Just as the hedgerows in the surrounding countryside fill with fruit so the heavily laden clusters of *Sorbus* berries ripen on the bough.

The effect is quite startling, from the familiar red berry of mountain ash, to the white berried *cashmiriana* and on to the amber-yellow of 'Joseph Rock', there are literally scores of different berry colours. For me one of the finest is *Sorbus hupehensis*. This is a beautiful small tree with large bluish-green leaves and white fruit tinged with pink, which hang in great drooping bunches like grapes on a vine. Close by, on Morley Ride can be found *Hibiscus syriacus* in full flower. This superb shrub, quite often referred to as 'Mallow', has large, rose pink, trumpet shaped flowers stained blood red in the centre. Reminiscent of Mediterranean regions it is a joy to discover on a warm sunny afternoon; such a wonderful sight but also a sad one for it heralds the end of summer.

Early morning mist obscures all but the great dome of Westonbirt House and in Silk Wood the delicate pink petals of meadow saffron, *Colchicum autumnale*, are damp from early morning dew. Great golden cotton reels of straw lay scattered across the surrounding agricultural lands, casting long shadows in the afternoon sun. That same mature sun lights up a mellow Cotswold stone wall by the greenhouses, providing a marvellous backdrop for the proud pink flowers of *Nerine bowdenii*. No fleeting flower display this, it will still be a joy when the first maples have turned colour, but that's another story, that is autumn. For the moment let's close our eyes, turn our face to the warmth of the sun and just once more listen to the soporific sounds of summer gently murmuring amongst the lime trees.

Overleaf 90-98. Tranquil Glades.

99. Golden berried mountain ash.

100. Cypress columns on Palmer Ride.

101. National Japanese maple cultivar collection.

99.

100.

101.

102. *Lime avenue in high summer.*

103. *Misty morning in Savill Glade.*

104. *Misty morning on The Downs.*

Opposite 105. *Summer leaves of the oriental plane.*

103.

104.

102.

Opposite 106. A shady corner of Savill Glade.

107. High summer in Leyshon Avenue.

108. Early morning on Mitchell Drive.

109. Summer's day in Silk Wood.

110. Late summer close to Old Acer Glade.

110.

109.

107.

108.

112.

113.

114.

115.

116.

117.

119.

118.

Opposite 120. Smoke bush flowers on Mitchell Drive.

121. Tree hydrangea with foxgloves.

122. Somewhere 'cool, green and shady'.

123. Laburnum and hawthorn flowers.

121.

122.

123.

125.

76

126.

127.

128.

129.

130.

131.

132.

135.

134.

133.

133. *Courtyard colour.*

134. *The Westonbirt Plant Centre.*

135. *Discovery!*

136. *A summer's morning by the Visitor Centre.*

Opposite 137. *A shady glade near Willesley Drive.*

136.

138.

139.

140.

141.

144.

145.

142.

143.

147. Nerine bowdenii.

148. Cornus kousa.

149. Lacecap hydrangea.

150. Indian bean tree flowers.

151. Leycesteria *flowers.*

152. Eucryphia *flowers.*

153. *Pocket handkerchief tree flowers.*

154. *Spindle fruits.*

155. *Chilean firebush flowers.*

156. *Tulip tree flowers.*

157. *Meadow saffron.*

158. *Mock orange blossom.*

159. Waste Drive in autumn.

AUTUMN

It was a foggy morning, and the trees shed in noisy water drops the moisture they had collected from the thick air, an acorn occasionally falling from its cup to the ground, in company with the dripping. In the meads, sheets of spider's-web, almost opaque with wet, hung in folds over the fences, and the falling leaves appeared in every variety of brown, green and yellow hue.

Thomas Hardy

161. *Downland maples and beech.*

Overleaf 160. October Glory.

AUTUMN – *Glorious Colours*

Early autumn days may be warm and sunny. If not for the encroaching darkness as the nights draw in, it could still be high summer. Gradually however, night-time temperatures begin to fall and these chilly nights, accompanied by early morning mists, bring Westonbirt to the golden threshold of another fall.

Mist hangs over cattle grazing on The Downs, their hot breath adding to the vapour that drifts between old parkland beech. Sodden gossamer threads stretch between wooden rails which protect young trees from browsing and the morning meanderings of the cattle are plotted on the moisture laden grass.

This is enough for some of Westonbirt's trees and shrubs to begin their autumn colour spectacular. Quietly at first, the tints are subtle, still masked by green. Then as the days shorten and the temperature falls, so the pace quickens and the shades intensify until, like some great symphony reaching its climax, the kaleidoscope of colour becomes almost overwhelming.

There is quite simply nowhere like Westonbirt in autumn. Every garden has its day, especially nature's own autumnal garden in the deciduous forests of North Eastern America, but for sheer intensity and brilliance Westonbirt in autumn is unsurpassed.

There are some experiences in life which stay with us forever. One such experience for me was my first visit to Westonbirt in autumn. It was many years ago now, long before I had the opportunity to help manage this marvellous collection. I came as a newly qualified Forester, expecting much, following the complimentary accounts delivered with such enthusiasm by lecturers, retired Foresters and a chance meeting with 'tree buff' Alan Mitchell.

However, nothing could have prepared me for that first view of the old maple glade. I had arrived late in the day, the sun was already below the afforested horizon of Silk Wood as I walked into the Old Arboretum. By the time I approached the glade, dusk was creeping in. Then, without warning, as I rounded a curve in the track, I saw the first Japanese maple. Perhaps it was the impending darkness, or the contrast provided by its proximity to a sombre yew, but it was as if each leaf shrouded a miniature red lantern. The colour was so intense I just stopped in my tracks convinced the foliage would burst into flame within seconds. I was not alone, others stood around in quiet admiration their faces glowing in its reflected glory. I then realised it was not one tree but a group of three, and there were others beyond beckoning me to come closer. For the next hour I stumbled across patches of darkness from one magnificent natural illumination to the next, from gold to copper, to pink, to crimson, and then finally to yellow. If anything the colours grew stronger as the last light in the sky faded, but if I had stayed any longer I would undoubtedly have caused myself injury. I reluctantly turned round and inched my way back through the blackness towards the car. It was a short visit, but one that even today quickens my pulse when I think of it.

Many years on from my first experience of a Westonbirt autumn I still feel a sense of excitement as autumn approaches. No two are ever the same, and each year I discover another jewel or perhaps another view of a well frequented autumnal friend.

One of the first trees to turn its leaves to autumn colour is the vine-leaved maple *Acer japonicum* 'Vitifolium'. Although comparatively rare in cultivation there are eleven specimens within the Westonbirt collection, including the tallest in Britain, standing alongside Main Drive and at some 12 metres tall, the variation in leaf colour is remarkable. In early September some of its leaves begin to change from summer green to yellow, then others develop patches of pink, crimson, gold and a beautiful deep ruby red. By early October the tree portrays every autumnal shade, with a smattering of green providing a delightful contrast. Finally, by late autumn those leaves left hanging on the branches turn purple before falling. It is a tree that will reliably produce a marvellous range of colours year after year. However, as with all autumn colouring trees some years the colour is more vivid than others.

The vine-leaved maple is a good early indicator as to what the autumn colours will be like in any given year. Every September beneath its canopy Westonbirt foresters can be seen gazing earnestly skyward trying to assess the probability of a vintage year. All around is an air of expectancy. One can almost feel the Arboretum holding its breath as the tree nervously displays its autumnal costume. The first outing of the season, will it be a success or just a pale imitation of some glorious past performance? Then with much nodding of heads and smiling, it is agreed, yes this is going to be a spectacular autumn, possibly the best for years.

Cool moist summers followed by a sunny September with one or two early ground frosts quite often produces the most vibrant colours. However, if the frosts are too severe, leaves will burn and fall before the colour change is complete.

The colouring of leaves in autumn is quite a complex subject, and still not fully understood. In simple terms, each leaf is a small food factory, processing water and minerals, transported to the leaf from the roots, and carbon dioxide obtained from the air, into plant food. The whole process is called photosynthesis. Energy for this process comes from sunlight which is trapped in the leaf within a green pigment called chlorophyll, it is this which gives the leaf its green colouring. Tree food is needed for growth, few trees grow in winter, so in autumn the food factory shuts down. The tree stops producing chlorophyll, and any left in the leaf slowly decays revealing other natural pigments, or autumn colours, previously hidden.

The trigger for this shutdown is provided by reducing temperatures and more importantly daylight hours. Although weather may vary dramatically throughout the year and effect colour intensity, the rate of reduction in daylight hours remains fairly constant. So the period of autumn colouring occurs at approximately the same time each year. At Westonbirt there are wonderful displays from mid-September until early November. However, it is in mid-October when the full glory of a Westonbirt autumn has to be seen to be believed.

On an early September day as the warm sun begins to melt away the morning mist, October seems a long way off. On Mitchell Drive butterflies skip between buddleia flowers watched by a gathering of swallows perched on the Downland fence noisily discussing their date of departure. Close by, an ancient pine tree has become the focus of attention for numerous bees and hoverflies. Its trunk covered with ivy in full flower providing a valuable source of early autumn nectar. Around this time a feeling of serenity settles on the Arboretum, a period of calm, with time to reflect. Time to store away those last few days stolen from summer, to be brought out like some well kept apple on a cheerless winter afternoon, when just the scent from its skin unlocks a flood of golden memories.

This quiet time is all the more poignant for we know it cannot last, the seasonal clock is changing and certainly we cannot stop it. Fruits dripping from every branch on spindle trees, *Euonymus* species seek to remind us of that. Beautiful deep pink capsules opening to reveal bright orange coated seeds inside are, like the vine-leaved maple, a sign that the performance is about to begin.

Suddenly from The Downs and picnic area close to the Visitor Centre comes the sound of children laughing and calling excitedly, for now is the time to search for conkers. Beneath the giant horse chestnuts, *Aesculus hippocastanum*, a group of children gather round a young boy proudly displaying the largest find. Such a treasure, and what a thrill as the outer casing falls away to reveal the large, rich brown, highly polished seed inside.

Autumn at Westonbirt is a wonderful time for children. There are so many fruits, seeds and leaves to collect of every colour, shape and size. So many collages to be made when their gleanings arrive back home or in the classroom. The Education Centre is in full swing during autumn with up to eight school parties a day using the indoor and outdoor classrooms. Where better to learn the basics of photosynthesis or woodland mammal habitats.

Education doesn't stop however when we leave school. There are numerous things to be learnt from this remarkable collection no matter what our age.

Throughout Westonbirt there are interpretative signs, waymarked walks and accompanying leaflets, explaining in more detail some facet of the Arboretum and its management.

One such walk is the Autumn Trail, which passes through some of the most spectacular autumn displays to be seen. The trail heads for Acer Glade, which by early October is stunning. As each day passes, so another crimson or gold brush stroke is added to this wonderful canvas of colour. To stand in the middle of Acer Glade on a bright afternoon with the sun shining through the canopy is quite magical. As each delicate cut leaf is illuminated by the sun's rays, it seems to catch fire, combining with its neighbours to set the whole glade ablaze.

There are literally hundreds of maples, (*acers*), in this area, including many cultivars of the Japanese maple, *Acer palmatum*. Along with *Acer japonicum* and its cultivars they provide the backbone of Westonbirt's autumn colour displays. Both have been cultivated for centuries in Japan, adapting well to the Japanese specialised style of gardening which includes Bonsai. Over the years, Japanese horticulturalists have selected and propagated more than two hundred different types, growing them in ornamental gardens and temple grounds. They reached their peak of popularity in Japan during the Edo era, 1603 - 1867.

Acer palmatum, the species, was first introduced into Britain in 1820, with many of its cultivars arriving over the following fifty years. By the 1870's the original, or 'old' Acer Glade had been planted at Westonbirt by Robert and Sir George Holford. A number of these trees still survive today, one hundred and twenty years old and in some cases still going strong. However, others have died or been lost in storms. The great gale of January 1990 caused widespread damage in this area but happily Westonbirt staff were able to successfully propagate from a number of the windblown specimens before they eventually died. Progeny from these are gradually being replanted around the Arboretum including the old Acer Glade area.

In the 1960's, soon after the Forestry Commission took over the management of Westonbirt, it became clear that to achieve continuity of autumn colour a new Acer Glade would need to be created. Trees do not live forever, and replacements should be planted long before they are required, thus allowing time for them to mature. So in anticipation of the old glade's demise a 'new' Acer Glade called Leyshon Avenue, was created alongside. To enhance the beauty of the new glade, seed was collected only from the most vibrant coloured *acers* in the old glade. Seedlings were raised and only those producing the strongest colours were selected for planting in the new glade, in some cases only two plants in every hundred were chosen.

Acer palmatum is particularly unpredictable when grown from seed. Almost every seedling will be slightly different to its parent. It may differ in leaf size, shape, tree form or autumn colour. A seed collected from a tree that turns a wonderful crimson in autumn may produce a seedling that turns an insipid rust colour. Alternatively it may be even more striking than the parent. It's a lottery, but what an exciting one, especially as any seed has the potential to turn into the finest coloured maple yet seen at Westonbirt.

Of those who visit in autumn, many go away with a Westonbirt maple seedling purchased from the Plant Centre. These are one year old seedlings and already give an indication of their autumn colour potential. Chosen carefully from the hundreds for sale, it is possible to create in the garden a little of the autumnal magic that is Westonbirt.

The Plant Centre is housed within a delightful old Cotswold stone barn, situated at the eastern end of the valley separating the Old Arboretum from Silk Wood. Just a couple of minutes walk from the main car park, it is well worth a stroll just to see inside the building. Plants are displayed amongst a wealth of old timbers and in the courtyard surrounding the barn, lichen covered dry stone walling provides a charming backdrop. Nothing could be further removed from the modern utilitarian garden centre and that goes for the plants too. Superb quality, replicating in miniature those wonderful specimens growing proudly within the Arboretum grounds.

One such group of proud specimens are little more than miniatures themselves. Sixty years old and still under two metres in height, but what they lack in stature they make up for in delicate foliage, graceful weeping habit and superb autumn colour. They are *Acer palmatum* 'Dissectum' the cut-leaved Japanese maple. Almost fern-like in appearance they can be found at the junction of Main Drive and Loop Walk, one of the first stops on the Autumn Trail. Attractive throughout the year, by mid-October they are quite dazzling, reminding one of the glowing embers from a series of bonfires.

Westonbirt is special at any time of the year, there are few places that evoke such feelings of tranquillity and serenity. One of the reasons for this is its size, at 600 acres Westonbirt is one of the largest arboreta in the world. So even on a mid-October afternoon, when the Autumn Trail is busy and admiring groups linger beneath every tree in Acer Glade, it is still possible to slip away to some secluded spot. This is one of the delights of Silk Wood, just a few minutes walk across the valley and one can feel the peacefulness descend.

In autumn, once beneath its mighty oaks, Silk Wood begins to reveal some quite astonishing displays of leaf colour hidden away from the main gravel paths.

One such area is The Link, a winding grass path that links Palmer Ride with Broad Drive. Along its length and off into the glades on either side are planted a fantastic array of Japanese maples. Although still quite young, planting started in the 1970's and is continuing today, these maples are already rivalling Acer Glade for the most spectacular display at Westonbirt. It is quite different to Acer Glade which has a somewhat formal landscaped appearance. Here, in The Link, the trees are scattered among natural woodland. It's as if some giant hand has cast hundreds of brilliant coloured jewels across the woodland. To watch them sparkling in the autumn sunshine, filtering through the latticework of branches overhead, is one of the greatest joys of a Westonbirt autumn.

To the west of The Link, on the far side of Broad Drive, is the official National Collection of Japanese Maple cultivars. Started in 1982 the collection now contains some 120 different cultivars and more are being added all the time. Eventually, it will also begin to rival the traditional areas of the Old Arboretum for colour display. Already the earliest plantings, now above head height, produce a delightful mixture of orange, red and gold. This collection has the advantage of being located adjacent to a plantation of Japanese larch, *Larix kaempferi*, which turns a rich gold in October. From a distance, when the sun shines, it looks like the maples are performing in front of a golden curtain. Most of these maple cultivars have Japanese names – Sango kaku, Beni shidare and Koto ito komachi. When translated they become almost as beautiful as the plants themselves – Coral Tower, Red Cascade and 'a beautiful girl with a harp of fine string'.

Another exotic sounding name is that of the Katsura tree, *Cercidiphyllum japonicum*, a native of China and Japan. A lovely graceful tree, producing delightful heart-shaped leaves which are bronzy pink when they first unfurl in spring. It is, however, in autumn when this tree really comes into its own. It can produce the clearest butter yellow leaf colour of any tree and if you are lucky enough to see them against an azure sky, the sight is unforgettable. Combined with this, in autumn the leaves emit a sweet fragrance similar to that of caramel or melting chocolate. The scent is quite elusive, it wafts through the air quite some distance from the tree and yet a crushed leaf in the hand may reveal little of this sugary delight. There are many groups of Katsura trees at Westonbirt, one of the finest is in an area called Colour Circle, close to Pool Avenue. This is a circle of some forty trees and shrubs quite deliberately chosen for the attraction of their autumn colour. Most of the trees were planted by the Holfords more than 100 years ago to create a venue for flamboyant Victorian parties. Tables laden with food would be set in the centre of the circle. The Holfords and their guests would then sit and sip champagne whilst admiring one of the most spectacular man-made landscapes of autumn colour in the world. It is good to know this is no longer the privilege of just a few, thousands of visitors stand in Colour Circle experiencing the beauty every year, who knows some may even sip their own champagne!

By late October the leaves are beginning to fall in ever increasing numbers, creating a wonderful patchwork of colour beneath and around each tree. Late autumn breezes mix and match those leaves lying on the ground creating delightful patterns of red, gold and purple of every shade imaginable. Children assist this process by kicking and shuffling through the crisp heaps of foliage searching for the finest specimens, which are then carefully placed in bags for future art work. Indeed, it is not only children, whether you are seven or seventy who can resist this leaf scattering occupation?

If the winds are strong and accompanied by heavy rain or hard frost the fall is sudden and over within days, as the colours fade so do the visitors. By early November those following the Autumn Trail have slowed to a trickle. The Arboretum breathes a long sigh, its final performance over it can now begin to prepare for winter. Leaves that fell early are already starting to decompose, releasing nutrients back to the soil, so important if the whole process is to begin again in little more than four months.

Gradually a silence descends. It is as if each individual plant is assessing its own part in the proceedings. Two months earlier on that sunny September day the vine-leaved maple had predicted a vintage year, it had indeed been right, the best anyone could remember. Standing under that same maple in early November, I wonder what next year will bring, its bare twigs give not a hint. Suddenly a cold wind speeds through from the open Downland, I fasten my collar. Long before next autumn, indeed between us and the spring, lies a Westonbirt winter, and that's an experience in itself.

171.

172.

173.

Opposite 174. Late autumn by Waste Gate.

175. 'Golden' maple on The Downs.

176. Autumn sunshine.

177. A golden day.

176.

177.

175.

180.

179.

178.

178. Japanese larch among the maples.

179. Leyshon Avenue.

180. Near the Autumn Trail.

181. Mid October in Old Acer Glade.

Opposite 182. 'The best seat in the house'.

181.

184.

104

185.

186.

187.

188.

189.

190.

191.

192. *Autumn glory.*

193. *'Just a glimpse of the house'.*

194. *Hickory and maple.*

Opposite 195. *'The backdrop'.*

193.

194.

192.

197.

198.

199.

200.

201.

202.

Overleaf   *196.*   *On the autumn trail.*

Opposite 197-202.   **Autumn shapes**
                   and colours.

      203-204.   **Either end of**
                   Specimen Avenue.

204.

203.

209.

Opposite 205. *'Beyond the glade'.*

206. *Looking out on Leyshon Avenue.*

207. *Close to Colour Circle.*

208. *'Contrasts'.*

209. *'Season of mists and moods'.*

208.

206.

207.

210. *Late September in The Link.*

211. *Autumn sunshine in The Link.*

212. *Shires return after 50 years.*

210.

211.

212.

215.

214.

213.

213. Autumn on The Downs.

214. Norway maple on The Downs.

215. Downland beech.

216. The fall begins in Lime Avenue.

Opposite 217. October afternoon.

Overleaf 218-229. A mosaic of autumn leaves.

216.

218.

219.

220.

221.

222.

223.

118

224.

225.

226.

227.

228.

229.

119

230. Waste Drive in winter.

WINTER

Oh, I remember now
A dell of snow,
Frost on the bough;
None there but I:
Snow, snow, and a wintry sky.
Walter de la Mare

232. Holford Ride.

Overleaf 231. The approach to Waste Gate.

WINTER – *Magical Landscapes*

Winter arrives at Westonbirt with little warning, or so it seems. Warmth from fiery autumn colours prevent even the thought of approaching winter to be considered until the last leaves have fallen. Then, as stinging rain brings a rouge to the cheek, one is shocked to realise the shortest day of the year is little more than a month away. Low pressure storms skud in from the Atlantic pushing before them blasting winds which rush up the Bristol Channel and throw themselves against the first high ground they encounter, The Cotswolds. On top of the wolds at 130 metres above sea level Westonbirt takes the brunt of these early winter storms.

On the open Downland it is difficult to walk against the wind and speech is stifled in the throat. The roar from this wind as it crashes through the great beech and black pine plantation on Beech Bank is quite awesome. Then, without warning the gusts subside, from across the valley in Silk Wood the creaking groan of a falling bough, ripped from a swirling head of oak, can be heard, and seconds later it crashes to the forest floor with a dull thud. Far away, probably in the swaying Douglas firs of Sand Earth, comes the hissing announcement of the next run of wind. The hiss gives way to a rumble and from the Downs one can follow its progress through Silk Wood by the tossing crowns on the far side of Palmer Ride. Suddenly, the wind breaks free of the woodland and rushes up the steep valley side towards the Old Arboretum. It is now that one fully appreciates the need for the matrix of shelter belts which cross through and surround the Arboretum. Planted by the Holfords, they contain trees and shrubs recognised for their wind resistance some 150 years ago. A sturdy mix of English and evergreen oak, yew, holly, laurel and box still providing protection today for the more tender exotic species on their leeward side.

The change in climate as one crosses the stile at Holly Bush Gate is quite remarkable. A few metres in from the boundary, on Circular Drive, the temperature has positively soared and the ferocious wind crossing the Downland outside is little more than a murmuring breeze as it filters through layers of dense foliage. In this sheltered environment three fieldfares are feasting on bright red fleshy fruits of yew (arils), and a lone blackbird walks back and forth across the path devouring fallen holly and cottoneaster berries. In the distance the hollow echoing call of a cock pheasant can be heard. Probably pleased with himself for remembering to pay a late afternoon visit to the bird tables adjacent to the Education Centre. A few more days of his gluttony and he in turn will provide a fine feast for the old dog fox padding past on his way out from his earth near Loop Walk. Dull winter afternoons are the best time to see some of Westonbirt's wildlife. They move more easily now, confidence growing as each day less visitors walk the grounds.

As dusk approaches so the wind eases and great rents appear in the heavy grey cloud cover, giving an occasional glimpse of the moon. By midnight most of the cloud has disappeared eastward, just the odd 'tail ender' scurrying past the bright silver moon. An owl calls from halfway up the tallest pine in Savill Glade and gradually the air temperature drops below freezing for the first time since March.

Night after night the temperature stays below freezing. After three nights of intense cold, daytime temperatures struggle to reach zero even though the sun shines out of the bluest of skies. In the evening, spectacular sunsets silhouette the bare latticework heads of Downland beach, etching every fine twig and thin bud against a glowing skyline which changes within minutes from orange to pink and then to purple. Gradually ice crystals build upon every branch clothing the Arboretum in a fine tracery of hoar frost, transforming dreary winter scenes into a stunning winter wonderland. Layers of glistening frost cover the upper surfaces of every individual evergreen frond and on Broad Drive fallen pine cones, their woody scales dusted with silver, look like the perfect Christmas decoration. On these bright frosty days there is a clarity, a sharpness to every vista. Trees previously growing in amorphous groups seem to separate out, their individuality heightened by a crisp white outline which traces every swirl and crook from mightiest trunk to finest sprig. Ice crystals creep between crevices and cracks on the rugged stems of ancient oaks in Silk Wood creating islands of bark like the joins of a jigsaw.

In the valley bottom the winter borne stream that has trickled past crimson, gold and lime-green stems of dogwoods and willows since early November has ceased to flow. A rivulet of ice lies in its place, glistening in the weak sun rays that only reach this shady spot for an hour or so in the middle of the day. At night cold air builds up in this valley and a dense foggy cloud climbs slowly up the valley sides, only to subside the following day as the sun reluctantly climbs above the overhanging trees of Silk Wood. Its limit is marked on the ground by frost covered grass like the tidal extremes of seaweed on the shore. This ponderous movement up and down the slope portrays the rhythmic breathing of winter. A slow and deliberate existence, patiently awaiting longer and warmer days which will quicken the pulse to the rhythm of spring.

In the depths of winter even the promise of spring can seem an age away. For some plants however, now is the time to open their precious flowers to the admiring gaze of those hardy souls striding across the iron hard ground on a brilliant winter morning.

Close to the Visitor Centre, where aromatic wood smoke lingers from the log fire burning brightly inside, sweet scented, delicate pink flowers of *Viburnum farreri* glisten in the sun and every stiff blade of grass sparkles with sugar frosting. No matter how hard or prolonged the frost may be, the Chinese witch hazel *Hamamelis mollis* will continue to flower. It has rich sulphur-yellow ragged flowers which are at their best in the depths of winter. There is no better tonic for a heavy heart at this time of year than the sight of the groups of witch hazels on Main Drive and in Savill Glade in full flower. Not only do they flower beautifully but as a bonus they provide the loveliest subtle fragrance imaginable.

On the western edge of Cherry Glade, curled, dull green leaves of Portuguese laurel, *Prunus lusitanic* hang lifeless from frigid branches and a frozen spiders web swings heavily in time to the cautious movement of a grey squirrel overhead. Close by, a winter flowering cherry – *Prunus subhirtell* 'Autumnalis' has braved the frost and thrust forward fragile, white petalled, flowers within a swollen pink bud. The peace and tranquillity in the glade is all encompassing. Other than my own breathing, the only other sounds come from the squirrel scratching and scrambling its way along the icy hazel branches on the edge of the woodland, occasionally joined by the echoing drumming of a greater spotted woodpecker searching for grubs beneath the bark of an old stag-headed birch. Both sounds seem to intensify the silence, it is easy to feel close to, indeed, part of nature at Westonbirt in winter.

It is now that many of Westonbirt's more subtle delights come to the fore. Eclipsed in other seasons by the showy displays of flowers and foliage, it is only in winter that one discovers the real beauty of bark. Once the eye is trained some of the best examples can be picked out from 50 metres away.

Undoubtedly one of the finest tree species for attractive bark is the Tibetan cherry, *Prunus serrula*. It is shiny and smooth, mahogany red in colour and looks as if it gets a good polish every day. I guarantee you will have difficulty restraining your hand from running up and down the trunk. If you are lucky enough to come across it gleaming in low winter sunshine you will know why it is considered to be one of the wonders of a Westonbirt winter, our best specimen is found at the Willesley Drive end of Palmer Ride.

Not far away on Broad Drive is a group of paper-bark maples, *Acer griseum*. Paper-bark because of the way the bark peels away in large papery flakes. Cinnamon in colour, they are at their best when seen against a foil of hoar frost or snow. There are further fine specimens on Mitchell Drive and Morley Ride. Crossing back over Broad Drive and heading down The Link, one soon discovers a stunning group of snake-bark maples, *Acer hersii*, with green and grey veining down the trunk they must be one of the most striking groups of maples in the whole of Silk Wood.

The Persian ironwood, *Parottia persica* has attractive cream and brown flaking bark, but in January it is the tiny flowers which catch the eye. Bright crimson in colour, they are no bigger than a small finger nail, but clustered together so abundantly on the branches, throughout its sprawling crown, that from a distance the whole tree takes on a reddish hue. It is well worth taking a closer look at these ruby flowers. Each collection of stamens is carefully protected in the bud by a chocolate brown velvety casing not dissimilar to moleskin. There are superb specimens of *Parottia persica* throughout Westonbirt including Colour Circle, Holford Ride and by Skilling Gate.

As each day of hard frost passes so more and more birds flock towards the Education Unit. Outside one of the classrooms a bird feeding area has been established. Every morning, seed, nuts, coconuts and water are put out as even the Dew Pond, adjacent to the Downs, is covered with thick bluey-grey ice, preventing any birds from drinking at its edge. Inside the classroom children excitedly cluster around the windows to watch as the birds swoop down to feed. Nuthatch, goldcrest, greater and lesser spotted woodpecker, greenfinch and treecreeper join the throng of more common garden birds. The children laugh as a tiny coal tit spars with its own mirrored image in the one-way glass. Clad in woolly hats and scarves these children will soon head out into the woods to discover more about the habitats of Westonbirt's bird population. As they leave the classroom and walk towards Main Drive many ask about the fragrance emanating from a number of low evergreen shrubs close to the path. With leathery dark green leaves similar to privet, they are ignored by the thousands who walk past for most of the year. However, those that pass in the weeks following Christmas are brought rapidly to a halt by this heady fragrance. The shrubs, *Sarococca humulis* and *ruscifolia* are the black and red berried Christmas box. It is hard to believe that such strong scent is produced by such tiny insignificant white flowers, but so it is and what an unexpected treat. The children crunch their way across crisp brown chestnut leaves, tapping their boots against rock hard mole hills as they go. Eventually their chatter is lost to the trees and once again a heavy silence descends, broken only by the rattling leaves, hanging from a young beech, as an easterly breeze stirs them into action.

Turning east one can see the mighty trunks of 'the three sisters' on the edge of Mitchell Drive. Three giant redwoods, *Sequoiadendron giganteum*, all over 35 metres tall and planted by Robert Holford's daughters, Margaret, Evelyn and Alice in 1865. Sadly both Margaret and Alice, struck by lightening in recent years, have lost their leading shoots. In time a side bud will produce another 'leader', however, due to their exposed position they are unlikely to grow much taller. Even on a dull day the colour of their thick fibrous bark is a rich, warm brown, but on this stunning winter afternoon as the sun drops towards a bank of cloud in the west, they are a radiant orange. For a few minutes they glow like beacons, then gradually the colour drains until only the very tops smoulder. Then, on each in turn, starting with Alice the smallest, the flame is snuffed, as the sun finally disappears behind yellowing clouds, it is destined not to return for quite some time.

That night the sound of water dripping from the woodland canopy is heard. Just one or two drops at first but by dawn it is like a steady rain. The thaw has arrived. Ice melting in the cracks of branches high in each crown trickles down through bark fissures. It joins forces with moisture from other branches until a small stream flows steadily down each trunk to soak into the softening ground at the base. Just after midday the first snowflake lands on the broad surface of a drooping rhododendron lead, slides off and falls to the woodland floor where it is lost within seconds. Before nightfall both rhododendron leaf and woodland floor lay thick with snow. A badger leaving its sett to visit its latrine, returns minutes later with a covering of glistening flakes on its back. It is snowing hard and shows no sign of easing.

The snow continues on and off for the next twelve hours and by silent daybreak even the most familiar landscapes of Savill Glade are hard to recognise. It has even become difficult to follow Main Drive. The weight of snow has pushed large clumps of bamboo across the path. The sight of bamboo covered with snow provides a rather surreal image, as does the glaucous blue-green leaves of a young *Eucalyptus gunnii*, emerging from a snowy blanket close to the Plant Centre. Some plants however, look far more at home, particularly the splendid Serbian and Brewers spruce, *Picea omorika* and *Picea breweriana* close to Willesley Drive. They originate from areas of high snowfall in Central Europe and North America, and have adapted well to their snowy homelands by developing drooping branches. They do not allow snow to lay heavily and cause breakage, the snow simply slides off the foliage to the ground. On this snowy day at Westonbirt one can almost see both trees smiling superiorly at a miserable evergreen oak, *Quercus ile,* which, no longer able to take the strain, shed two large limbs during the night.

Without doubt some of the highlights of a snowy day at Westonbirt are the groups of red dogwood, *Cornus alba 'Sibirica'* found throughout the Arboretum. The four groups at Scots Corner, where Holford Ride and Pool Avenue meet, look particularly magnificent. Great swathes of intense crimson stems thrusting upwards from the snow clad ground. This contrast is so vivid, after a while my sense of balance is affected and I turn away to look down the length of Holford Ride towards Westonbirt School. What an age ago it seems since I stood on this spot, one hot July day, watching the great domed roof of the school shimmering in the distance. Today, the roof is barely visible, but the creamy yellow stone of the walls stands out sharply against the pure white snow.

Across the ride the seat, that in summer was surrounded by a young family having a picnic, can now hardly be seen. Only the vertical wooden uprights of the backrest are free from snow. It adds to the deep sense of solitude, which I have felt since leaving my office. To the left of the seat is another conifer resplendent in the wintry weather. It is the golden Scots pine, *Pinus sylvestris 'Aurea'*, which for most of the year has dull bluey-green needles. In January however they take on a glorious golden tint that lifts the tree into a class of its own. There are smaller specimens on Palmer Ride, but the tree on Holford Ride contrasting so well against the dark green foliage of a neighbouring Douglas fir, is without doubt the finest specimen at Westonbirt.

A sudden frantic clapping from the wings of a wood pigeon, startles me from my reverie. Knocked from its roost by a small avalanche of snow dislodged by two fieldfares, the pigeon flaps urgently skywards. I turn and scrunch my way across virgin snow towards Pool Gate and the light across the Downland shining out from the Visitor Centre.

The snow hangs heavy on each bough for five days. On the morning of the sixth day, the eastern sky is aglow as the rising sun reflects off the low cloud overhead and the wintry landscape warms with a soft pink flush. The red coat of a lone fox, pausing to sniff the air by a battered old cedar in Jackson Avenue, positively gleams. The fox turns and pads away back to its earth and mate, feeling sure rain will arrive shortly and with it the end to the worst of the winter weather.

By early February the last snow has disappeared. It lingered for quite some time, particularly beneath a group of upturned windblown conifer stumps in the wildwood between Holford and Morley Ride. Waiting, some said, for company from further snowfalls. None came, and slowly, almost reluctantly, the snow dwindled away. For a while the winter borne stream, swollen with melt water, flowed steadily past the lichen covered Cotswold stone walls of the Plant Centre. However, by the time the catkins on the overhanging branches have begun to lengthen, this too had virtually disappeared.

At last there is a noticeable increase in daylight hours and the sun begins to penetrate those dark shady corners of Silk Wood, which have not seen sunlight since October. On the acid soil areas of Savill Glade and Sand Earth, stout olive-green camellia and rhododendron buds begin to swell, confirming that winter is indeed on the wane. Close to Skilling Gate, a cornealian cherry, *Cornus mas* is covered with yellow blossom, which has burst forth from yellowish-green leafless twigs. It almost dares the winter to return with a vengeance, as indeed it might. Whatever happens now though will be short-lived, already the dark brown earth on the area of hazel, coppiced last year, is beginning to green up. Fleshy rosettes of narrow leaves mark the spots from which delicate nodding white snowdrop heads have begun to appear. It has been a long winter, and a hard one, but, that in itself has enabled Westonbirt's vast collection of trees and shrubs to put on a stunning display of winter colour. Dramatic and graceful shapes of bare trees with patterned and coloured bark have provided images that will stay etched on my memory until I reach my own wintertime.

At Westonbirt six hundred years ago, the first hazel stem was cut in deepest winter. Today that same hazel is being re-coppiced. Within two months the cut stump will sprout green shoots in the gentler climate of spring and the seasonal cycle of life will begin once more.

Overleaf 233-241. Magical Landscapes.

    242. Across the valley.

    243. January in The Link.

    244. Japanese maples.

242.

243.

244.

245. *The national Japanese maple cultivar collection.*

246. *Late winter in The Link.*

247. *'As evening approaches'.*

Opposite 248. *February in The Link.*

246.

247.

245.

132

Opposite 249. *A fine tracery of hoar frost.*

250. *'A snowy glade'.*

251. *'The seat'.*

252. *Leyshon Avenue in winter.*

253. *Across to beech bank.*

253.

252.

250.

251.

255.

256.

257.

258.

259.

260.

Overleaf 254. Winter wonderland.

Opposite 255-260. Winter bark.

261-262. Bark detail.

262.

Opposite 263. Japanese maple on Willesley Drive.

264. Beech in early winter.

265. Early winter near Old Acer Glade.

266. 'Time to reflect'.

264.

265.

266.

270.

269.

268.

271.

144

273.

274.

275.

276.

277.

278.

279.

280.

281. *Winter evergreens.*

282. *The valley bottom.*

283. *A winter's day on The Downs.*

281.

282.

283.

284.

284. 'Contrasts' on Holford Ride.

285. Pollarded willows.

286. 'Just a dusting'.

Opposite 287. Scarlet willow.

Overleaf 288. In the depths of winter.

285.

286.

PHOTOGRAPHIC NOTES

For me, photography is about light, colour, the right moment and magic.

Sometimes when the right light, colours and opportunity come together you really can find magic. It can be at any time, in any weather and surprisingly when the least expected. It will appear, sometimes for a few minutes, sometimes longer – you must be ready and let it happen. When it does appear, it is like some very special gift, presented on a beautiful stage – it is Nature.

Some places have this special magic. Westonbirt is such a place, it has a spiritual and special quality that is hard to define but if you can let your eyes and heart be open you will find it. When you do, you will be as close to Nature as you can get. The hard, impossible part is trying to capture that quality and feeling on film and sharing it with others.

I don't think of myself as a photographer, I just take photographs in an effort to capture the beauty, the moment and the wonder of nature – I am reminded of the words of John Clare, the countryside poet – "I didn't write the poems I found them in the fields". If you can take time and become one with your environment you will find more pictures than you can imagine ....

> "The path my feet took was lined with images, whole gardens of pictures. With exposures I picked bouquets, each more vivid than the previous .... finally a gathering of gem-like flames in the low tide ... I thought I had forgotten how to use my camera, so I counted each step of the process aloud ... shutter speed, aperture, cock the shutter ... Though I feared to lose the sense of beauty, no less occurred; the sense of rapport was strong beyond belief."

From "Rites & Passages" by Minor White. Published by Aperture, Inc. N.Y.

You may be wondering what practical help I can be – but first for me is a state of mind, being able to be at one with the countryside, landscape or garden, being able to really see and feel Nature. Shutter speeds and "F" numbers are not part of my conscious record – they are just information from the light meter which is transferred to the camera at that moment and is special and relevant only to that moment and time.

My most important photographic equipment is a strong tripod, giving me time to compose and consider, a polarizer filter to cut out unwanted reflections and improve colour, (the cheapest and most effective way to improve landscape and garden photography) and a cable release.

The only other accessory that would improve your photography would be a Mobile Home. With this you would be able to go to sleep and wake up with the dawn in your chosen location. That is my idea of Heaven.

Derek Harris. April 1995.

I would like to thank FUJI for Professional film, and finally my thanks for the first class service and E6 processing from Eric Carr of 42 Bluebell Avenue, Peterborough, PE1 3XQ.

ACKNOWLEDGMENTS

We should like to thank Forestry Commission, Forest Enterprise staff who gave help and advice in the preparation of this book.

Our heartfelt thanks to all Westonbirt staff members for their support and enthusiasm. Special thanks must go to Jane Smith and Margaret Ruskin for their dedication and patience during the preparation of the typescript and to Hugh Angus for his support and assistance.

To His Royal Highness, The Prince of Wales for his splendid Foreword.
To Rosemary Verey for her encouragement and delightful words.
To J.D.Vertrees for translations from his book "Japanese Maples".

To Penguin Books for the reproduction of the poems of Thomas Hardy and D.H.Lawrence. Michael Joseph Ltd. for the reproduction of the George Meredith poem and to J.M.Dent and Sons for the reproduction of the Walter de la Mare poem. To Aperture, Inc. N.Y. for the Minor White Quotation.

Tony Russell and Derek Harris.
April 1995.

My personal thanks also to Esther Marshall for her help and encouragement.
To Chris Richardson and all at Goodfellow & Egan in Peterborough who worked on the Origination and Typesetting for their support and interest in the preparation of this book.

And finally to Henry David Thoreau, Ralph Waldo Emerson, Walt Whitman, John Burroughs and Jean Giono for their inspiration and wonderful words.

Derek Harris.
April 1995.

The ten hours' light is abating,
And a late bird wings across,
Where the pines, like waltzers waiting,
Give their black heads a toss.

Beech leaves, that yellow the noon-time,
Float past like specks in the eye,
I set every tree in my June time,
And now they obscure the sky.

And children who ramble through here,
Conceive that there never has been
A time when no tall trees grew here,
That none will in time be seen.

Thomas Hardy

158

"The true harvest of life is intangible. It is as the tints of morning and evening. It is a little stardust caught .... a segment of the rainbow."...........